Rainbow Stories

KETHA ANURADHA

© **Ketha Anuradha 2022**

All rights reserved

All rights reserved by author. No part of this publication may be reproduced, stored in a retrieval system or transmitted in any form or by any means, electronic, mechanical, photocopying, recording or otherwise, without the prior permission of the author.

Although every precaution has been taken to verify the accuracy of the information contained herein, the author and publisher assume no responsibility for any errors or omissions. No liability is assumed for damages that may result from the use of information contained within.

First Published in November 2022

ISBN: 978-93-5668-339-6

BLUEROSE PUBLISHERS
www.BlueRoseONE.com
info@bluerosepublishers.com
+91 8882 898 898

Cover Design:
Muskan Sachdeva

Typographic Design:
Pooja Sharma

Distributed by: BlueRose, Amazon, Flipkart

Preface

Dualities are everywhere: happiness and distress, honor and dishonor, pleasure and pain, success and failure, victory and defeat, health and disease, beautiful and ugly. Whatever the circumstances, we should always look for a positive opportunity to grow. Only light can dispel darkness, and happiness can overcome heartbreaking sadness. A healthy tree has strong roots and can survive storms and hurricanes. Similarly, a strong spiritual foundation is required to sustain all of life's duplicities.

Some people call these dichotomies "black and white." White contains all colors and black excludes all. In reality, life is like a box of crayons, and we should paint the canvas of our life with the whole box. Be a rainbow and celebrate life with the colors of love, kindness, compassion, gratitude, courage, satisfaction, integrity, respect, sacrifice, truthfulness, austerity, and authenticity.

Dedication

To my dear daddy

Dr. P.V.Rao

For all the fairy tales, I grew up reading

Contents

Virtues And Vices 1

A Friend And A Mother 7

Grandpa Grandma 11

Rich And Wealthy 17

Shield And Weapon 22

Loneliness And Solitude 26

Be Unreasonable 32

Lead The Way 37

Think, Don't Judge 41

Wealthy And Happy 45

Contribution And Competition 50

Legacy And Legitimacy 57

Ambition, Fame, And Success 62

Indulgence And Prudence 67

Visible And Invisible 72

Pleasure And Happiness 76

Facts And Opinions 80

Best Friend 85

Virtues And Vices

It was eight o'clock in the morning. Hearing the doorbell, Dr. Anita Mahajan, rushed to open the door with the coffee mug in her hand. The Morning bell is music to the ears when the housemaid is being expected. "What happened, Savitabai?", she asked sympathetically on seeing her bruised face and swollen eyes. "Nothing madam. I slipped on the muddy road yesterday while going back home," she replied, trying to hide her emotions, and put on a brave face. Dr. Anita sensed something was wrong and silently gave her medicine. Savita had been working as a housemaid for the Mahajan family for the last ten years. Dr. Anita was a gynecologist, and her husband was a cardiologist. The couple trusted her to take care of the household chores in their absence. They treated her kindly. A self-respecting lady, Savita would only talk about her twin sons and hardly mention her violent, drunkard husband.

Savita lived in a shanty hut with her husband Sitaram and her two sons - Luv and Kush. A few years back, Sitaram was working as a watchman in a gated community, but he was highly irregular, and his services were terminated. Sometimes, he would bring heaps of scrap from outside for sorting. One evening, after returning from work, Savita found the scrap lying on the floor. "When will you finish the sorting?", she asked him. Without cleaning, they could not go to sleep. Sitaram did not respond and continued drinking. Tired after a day's work, Savita asked him politely to clear the scrap, so that she could mop the floor for everybody to sleep on. Inebriated, he started shouting and abusing her. Silently, she and her two sons dumped everything in a bag, cleaned the floor, and retired for the day. Incidents like this occurred frequently in the house.

Sitaram had no regard for his wife, never bothered to help her but was adept at passing demeaning comments. The twins grew up amidst all the domestic violence. Every day in the morning, Luv would get up himself and fetch milk for tea and other groceries for the day. But Savita had to wake up Kush, "Kush, get up. There is already a long queue at the water pump." Kush would pull the soiled blanket over his face and say, "One minute, Maa." Reluctantly and yawning, half-awake Kush would fetch water, which was used for cooking and cleaning utensils. Savita cooked for the family and rushed to work, hoping for a peaceful atmosphere to welcome her on her return.

Luv and Kush were twins with different personalities. Luv was silent, observant, obedient, and sympathetic towards his mother. Kush was notorious, rowdy, and indifferent to his mother's sufferings. Luv had a passion for learning, excelled in academics, and was a consistent top scoring student in his school. As he could not study peacefully in his own home, he found solace in the nearby ISKON temple. It was like a second home to him. Swamiji and other staff members fondly called him, 'Chotu'. He would run errands for the Swamiji. He rendered help to the staff in various activities like cleaning the floor, moving benches from one hall to another, and managing the crowd. He found comfort and inspiration in

Swamiji's talks. Meditation sharpened his mind and promoted his emotional health. It improved his self-image and concentration.

Savita was always worried about Kush. He became very friendly with a boy from a local gang. He started absconding from school and used to hang out on the streets with his friends. They wandered, cracked jokes, imitated movie dialogues, and sang songs. Slowly, even more notorious boys joined the group, and the group grew in number. Constantly being rebuked at home and being compared to his twin brother, he gravitated towards friends who did not hold him accountable for his behavior He did what other members were doing- shoplifting, defacing property, using drugs, and drinking. He even got arrested a couple of times. He was a constant source of worry to his mother.

One Sunday afternoon, while giving her mistress a head massage, she asked, "Madam, you are a gynecologist. Please tell me how it is that my sons, who share the same birth charts, have such different personalities. "Dr. Anita replied, "Apart from genes, the environment also plays a significant role in shaping the personality of the child. Children compete for their parents' love, attention, and time in a family. Luv excels in academics and both of you are proud of him. Kush is consciously or unconsciously trying to develop his expertise in socializing. Due to ill luck, he has fallen into bad company."

She continued, "The violent and turbulent atmosphere at home has a different impact on different children. Luv has sought refuge in Swamiji and imbibed all virtues. Kush drifted away and developed all the vices. The group gives him a sense of belonging that was not there for him at home. All children need to be nurtured with love, affection, care, and understanding to grow up as responsible adults. Kush is a sensitive soul. He craves your appreciation and recognition. Savita started sobbing, "What can I do, Madam? My husband only fights the whole day."

Tenth-standard results were declared. Luv topped his school. Dr. Anita helped Luv in securing admission to a reputed college. Due to financial constraints, Luv opted for Arts instead of engineering and science. He aimed to crack the Civil Services Examination one day. The other students in his class were from wealthier families, and some of them used to make fun of his slum background. He said to himself, "This is a temporary phase. This too shall pass." He remembered Swamiji's advice, "Your thoughts play a significant role in shaping your future." So, he only dreamt of the day he would become an IAS officer, spent hours in the college library, and paid no heed to the nuisance makers. Meanwhile, his father's health deteriorated due to alcoholism, and he passed away. Savita was now even more obsessed with Kush's future. She would keep asking Luv, "Kush is never at home. Why don't you ask him to mend his ways?"

Persistent questions about Kush sometimes irritated Luv. He would reflect, "Why she never enquires about me after coming home? It is always Kush and Kush." In a family, parents usually tend to worry more about children who are weak in their studies or are facing other issues in their lives. Other children sometimes start to feel neglected. Savita loved both her sons dearly, but she was more concerned about Kush and his future. She had full faith in Luv that he would be successful in life. But the child in Luv craved his mother's concern. He shared his feelings with Swamiji. He told him to take pride in the fact that he was not the source of worry for his mother. Otherwise, his mother would have been burdened with the uncertain future of her two sons. He chided him not to let such thoughts poison his mind and to focus on his studies.

Finally, Luv cleared the Civil services examination with an All-India Rank of 21. Overnight, he became a celebrity. He was chased by the media and felicitated by his school and college. His mother's joy knew no bounds. She thanked God for answering her prayers. Luv was posted in one of the districts as a Subdivision Magistrate. They all happily lived together in his official accommodation, a huge bungalow with household help such as cooks, gardeners, and drivers. For Savita, all this was nothing less than a fairy-tale come true. She was grateful to the Almighty. Her son was reaping the rewards of his hard work.

Savita was also happy that Kush was away from bad company. He spent the entire day watching television, strolling in the garden, and sleeping. Whether Kush was proud or envious of him, Luv could never understand. Luv wanted to engage Kush in some activity. One day, while buying notebooks for his personal use, he had an epiphany. He went home and talked to his mother, "Kush is just whiling away his time. We can open a stationery shop for him, and you can assist him." When the family sat down for dinner, Luv asked Kush if he would like to be a stationery shop owner. Kush happily agreed, and Savita blessed both her sons.

On the auspicious day of Gudipadwa, "Kush stationery" was inaugurated. After giving instructions to the servants for the day, Savita had ample time to help Kush. Apart from stationery, the shop had inspirational books like 'Amar Chitra Katha', 'Panchatantra', 'Mahabharat', 'Ramayana' etc. When the customers were not around, Kush started reading these books. This enriched his mind with moral values. He realized his follies. He had not chosen good company. He tried to unlearn everything he had absorbed till then and tried to imbibe good moral values.

Savita was happy with this transformation. She would proudly tell everybody, "I am a proud mother of two virtuous twins with the same birth charts."

A Friend And A Mother

Feeling happy and excited, Seema was distributing sweets among her colleagues in the Physics department of Junior College. When she knocked at Madhuri Madam's cabin, she got a burlesque reply, "Come in." Seema offered her sweets, "Madam, I got my confirmation letter today." Prof. Madhuri looked nervous when she congratulated her. A few books were scattered on her table. Seema expressed her concern and asked, "Madam, Can I help you?" Madhuri said, "Actually, my mother-in-law has been hospitalized and I was unable to come to the college for the past few days. Today, I have to deliver a lecture on - *The Theory of Relativity*, a new topic that has been introduced in the syllabus for the first time. Seema, a Gold Medallist in Physics, calmed her nerves by lucidly explaining the topic. Madhuri was quite impressed with her subject knowledge and pedagogy. Madhuri invited Seema to join her for lunch, and from that day onwards, they started meeting every day for lunch and evening tea. In a very short time, they became very good friends.

The students revered and loved Madhuri madam for her strong personality and amiable behavior. Apart from academics, she motivated and encouraged students to follow their dreams. Seema secretly admired the way Prof. Madhuri had built her rapport with the students. Usually aloof and reticent, Seema knew deep down that she would never be able to do all this. Seema was acclaimed for her subject expertise and high-quality teaching. She always helped the students when they approached her for assistance and suggestions. She would try to make the topics interesting by giving real-life experiences.

Madhuri was happily married and had a two-year-old son, Prateik. Hailing from a close-knit family, her brothers and sisters lived nearby. They simply enjoyed being around one another and were there for each other to weather life's changes and challenges. Frequently, they would all go on vacations and Madhuri would show the albums to Seema, introducing her to her strong, lovely family. Seema was impressed by the strong bond shared by the family members.

Madhuri and Seema were organizing a Science Exhibition. Unfortunately, the student who was making the posters had an accident and other students were busy with their projects. Seema suggested, "Madhuri Madam, you can come to my place, and we can finish the work together in one day." Seema lived in a huge bungalow with her parents. The servant guided Madhuri to Seema's room and silently served them tea and snacks. There were no greetings exchanged. The silence in the home was deafening.

Both worked with full concentration and finished their work quickly. Before leaving, Madhuri expressed her wish to meet her parents and thank them. Her mother was supervising the servant who was arranging the crockery. Seema introduced her to her mother, "Mom, this is Madhuri, my friend and colleague." With folded hands, Madhuri greeted her, "Namaste Auntyji. Thanks for the tea and snacks." Her mother replied, "Namaste beta" and continued giving instructions to the servant. Her father was engrossed in a book, and he just nodded his head when she greeted him. Madhuri could sense the emotional void in Seema's life and the reason for her aloofness. She mused, "Seema never talks about her family."

High in emotional intelligence and life skills, Madhuri always focused on boosting the dormant self-esteem of the students. Seema, on the other hand, was acclaimed for her academic intelligence. They enjoyed many meaningful conversations and had a lot to teach and learn from each other. One day, Madhuri reminisced and shared some childhood incidents, "In our family, every occasion is an excuse for a celebration. Even though we were not very rich, my parents ensured that we had a happy childhood. We did not have lavish birthday parties, but we had a small gathering of friends and neighbors. They all relished the lip-smacking delicacies doled out by my mother. We frequently went for picnics and had fun-filled family times." Many times, Madhuri talked at length about her family hoping Seema would confide in her about her family issues. But Seema kept her secret sacred. She remembered reading somewhere, "Do not reveal your family issues to others. People are more interested in rubbing salt on your wounds rather than applying the balm."

The night before going to sleep, she pondered over her childhood and tears welled up in her eyes thinking about all that she did not get from her parents. Painfully, she recollected, "My parents never acknowledged, validated, or responded to my feelings. They never abused me, but they never made me feel special. Cool and rejecting, they never comforted me or celebrated my achievements." Socrates rightly expounded, "The unexamined life is not worth living."

It dawned on her that her parents' failure to provide an emotional response was playing out in a big way in her life. Her feelings had been ignored for so long that she could not connect with people. She found solace in reading and buried herself in books. She was a voracious reader and devoured books on child emotional neglect. One day, she visited her aunt and poured her heart out, "I fail to understand why my mother never expressed her love or concern for me. My feelings were always dismissed. There was no celebration even when I topped the university." Her aunt understood her plight, took her hands in her own hands, and said lovingly, "My dear child, your mother, Nalini had a troubled childhood. Nalini's father, who happens to be your grandpa, always craved a son, and he neglected his wife. Nalini's mother went through a lot of emotional turmoil, and your mother grew up unloved and unwanted."

After learning about her mother's childhood, Seema was able to put the puzzle pieces together and had a crystal-clear image of everything. Her mother herself had grown up without sufficient emotional mothering. How could she give her something which she had not received? She started putting all her emotions in a journal, let go of all the pain, and forgave her mother. Her best friend, Madhuri, became a maternal figure to her.

Emotional hurt, grudges, and jealousy can make our minds toxic. Our body has a system to remove unwanted food, water, or air without our awareness. How we wish there was an automatic arrangement that could throw away negative feelings and emotions as well.

Grandpa Grandma

"Dadaji, Dadaji, get up. I want to go to the garden," ten-year-old Preeti was pulling her grandfather's arms. Ashok quickly got up, had his evening tea, and they left for the garden. Very often, Preeti could be seen holding her grandfather's hands while going for a walk and he was known as "Preeti's Dadaji." Not only the children, but the garden was also a favorite gathering place for grandmas, grandpas, parents, and maids. While the children played merrily in the garden, Ashok along with other grandpas engaged in various fun activities such as singing, sharing jokes, and yoga. On returning home, they were served a cold banana milkshake by her grandma and Preeti rushed to her room. She always completed her homework before her parents came back from work. In their home, there was a protocol that after dinner, there would be no office calls or meetings. One hour before going to bed was family time where they would share their experiences of the day.

Preeti's parents were working for a private airline. Her grandparents were her best buddies. While her parents were involved in their daily struggles, her grandparents seemed to be always relaxed, calm, and patient. They always had time to talk to her and made her feel special. Every day in the morning, her grandmother, along with Kavitabai, made her favorite snacks for the school tiffin. When she returned home, they would enquire about her school, friends, and teachers.

Grandma, "How was the cheese sandwich I made for you? Did you share it with your friends? "

"No, grandma, it was delicious and my favorite one.

I did not feel like sharing it with anybody."

"No beta, you should always share your tiffin with others."

Grandparents hold a special place in the lives of their children's children. They play with them, spoil them, and indulge in ways they would not indulge their children. They cheered for all her accomplishments, whether big or small. Grandpa would proudly announce to everyone, right from the morning milkman and driver to the security guard, "Our beti won a gold medal." He was a simple, jolly man. He was liked by all, and they congratulated him. Every day, he greeted them and enquired about their welfare. Her grandmother would call her friends and cousins and spout her achievements. All this boosted her confidence and motivated her to perform better. For grandparents also, the feeling of authority and responsibility kept them active and healthy.

Preeti's mother, Neelam, was very fastidious about personal hygiene and cleanliness. She ensured that the house was always spotless. One could frequently hear her reprimanding Preeti, "Preeti, brush your teeth. Preeti, clean your room. Why is your book lying on the sofa in the living room?" One day, Grandpa overheard Neelam shouting at Preeti for not arranging her books properly in the cupboard. He immediately rushed to her rescue. He said, "She had organized her cupboard properly. I only ransacked the cupboard searching for glue." Then he smiled mischievously at Preeti and winked at her. From his own life experiences, he learned that life is too short to worry about such petty issues. Parents don't have time to deal with children and tend to discipline them, but grandparents communicate the same thing differently and more convincingly.

Her parents used to take a break from their hectic schedules. Airlines offered discounted flights to the entire family, and they traveled to distant locations. They used this opportunity to relax and spend quality time with their daughter. Her grandparents owned a farmhouse on the outskirts of the city. They used to spend their long weekends there. Preeti loved that huge bungalow surrounded by trees, listening to the chirping of birds, touching soft grass, and beautiful flowers. Travel gave her global exposure. She interacted with people from different backgrounds and developed excellent communication skills.

Even on the days when her parents had to go to the office, but her school was closed, her days were fun packed. Her grandmother loved cooking, and Kavitabai assisted her. Grandpa mostly watched television or read newspapers. Preeti had never seen her grandpa in the kitchen. One day, she asked him, "Dadaji, why is it that only Dadi works in the kitchen, and you never help her?" His children could never talk to him like that. Unlike parent-child relations, grandfather-grandchild relations are very simple. He grinned, " I am a retired person." The word "retirement" did not exist in Grandma's dictionary. She believed one should never retire in life and always serve others. Along with her grandma, Preeti would also cook using her toy kitchen set, feed her doll, and lullaby her to sleep. She also had a huge collection of toy cars. Grandpa had taught her the car brands and their logos.

Together, they would race the cars and play video games. Her grandmother had worked as a professor of English literature and would tell her stories with moral values.

In her class, while other students mingled and chatted, there was one girl named Anuja, who remained aloof and silent. Her father was an eminent politician, and she used to come to school in a chauffeur-driven limousine with a gun-wielding guard. Her reticence was misinterpreted as arrogance. One day, Preeti happened to have lunch with her. Anuja's sandwiches were burnt, and she hardly ate anything. Preeti shared her paneer Franky with her. Anuja said, "My mother has gone to Delhi for a business meeting. The maid was using the toaster for the first time." Her mother was an entrepreneur and a socialite. Preeti felt sad that Anuja was usually alone in the house.

While driving back home, Preeti remembered the time when her grandparents had gone on a ten-day trip. She had cried herself hoarse. After coming back from school, Kavitabai served her snacks. She missed her grandparents and sulked in her room. One weekend, her parents took her for a picnic. On the calendar, she would put a cross on each passing day. Even her grandparents could not stay away from her. They curtailed their trip and returned. On her return from school one day, she was pleasantly surprised when her grandfather opened the door. She jumped and clapped and ran into his arms. She kissed them fervently and said, "I am so happy you are back." "We also missed you, darling." An old Indian proverb says, "For grandparents, grandchildren are like cream of milk."

One day, she told her grandma about Anuja. She told her,

" Why don't you invite her to your birthday party?" At the party, Anuja sat quietly in one corner. Her grandmother talked to her lovingly. After the party, she said, "The child is emotionally disturbed. She is feeling neglected. She holds a grudge against her parents for not being there for her." Anuja liked the warmth and loving atmosphere of Preeti's home and started visiting them frequently. One evening, they invited her parents for tea. While they were discussing such things, her grandparents emphasized Anuja's well-being. "Both of you have very hectic schedules, and you are not able to spend quality time with your daughter. She craves your love and affection." Anuja's parents realized that they were satisfying their daughter's materialistic needs but not her emotional needs.

As the business was well established, Anuja's mother delegated her work to others and started supervising from home. Video conferencing and web cameras helped her stay connected with her staff and monitor every activity. Sometimes, she would drop her daughter at school and rush to attend board meetings. Three pm was a Flintstones whistle for her, and she would wind up everything and leave for Anuja's school. On the way, she would ask about her day at school and share her own experiences. She treasured every moment spent with Anuja and drew immense satisfaction from being there for her daughter. Her perspective toward work changed and she became more empathetic and considerate towards her employees. She introduced flexible working hours for her employees, and they too started working with increased dedication, and the productivity of the company increased. Anuja metamorphosed into a vibrant and confident girl. Anuja and Preeti became best friends and gradually, Anuja became popular among the students.

Family is the most important influence in a child's life. It provides security, identity, and value to them.

Rich And Wealthy

Gautam banged on the door of his room, venting out his anger on the punching bag with loud music blaring out of it. His friend, Pankaj, was going on a cruise holiday to Goa. After having slogged for the full year for his Higher Secondary Examinations, he felt entitled to relax and unwind. All his pleas were repudiated by his father in a stern voice. "There are rave parties and illicit drug activities are carried out on these luxury liners. At this vulnerable age, you should not go unless accompanied by some elderly people. Any unpleasant incident will leave you scarred for the rest of your life." His father, Mr. Nilesh Gupta, was the Vice-president of a reputed international tour and travel company and had taken his family to beautiful destinations across the world. His son's adamant behavior puzzled him.

One day, Mr. Nilesh was discussing an outdoor corporate activity for a multinational company with Mr. Alok Jain, manager at the event management company. Mr. Alok had a flamboyant style-signature wristwatch, a gold necklace, and the latest cellphone. Mr. Alok suggested activities like team cooking, drumming, and Karaoke, and Mr. Nilesh was quite impressed by these innovative and out of the box ideas. While finalizing the finer details of the program over lunch, they discovered, to their utter surprise, that they were classmates. Nilesh recollected that during school days also, Alok was known for flaunting his possessions—latest electronic gadgets and expensive toys.

During school days, both wanted to do something adventurous and exciting in their lives and not follow in the footsteps of engineers and doctors. Alok reminisced his journey so far, "After doing my Diploma in Resort and Hotel Management, I worked as a resort manager before joining this company." Nilesh pointed to a framed photograph on his table and said, "What a lovely family! It has been a wonderful experience working with you." Alok tried to break the ice by asking, "Have you realized that we are meeting after three decades? Your visiting card says you are an IIM alumnus. I am proud of you. Let us meet with our families over dinner." So, they started going for family picnics and Alok's son Pankaj and Gautam became close friends.

Like his father, Pankaj was also a braggart. Whenever Gautam visited Pankaj at his place, he would be dazzled by the magnificent living room, plush sofas, Persian carpets, paintings, and artifacts collected from across the world. Young Gautam failed to understand and wondered, "How do these people lead such an opulent lifestyle? My father holds a prestigious position, and still we live modestly." Everything went fine till the Novel Coronavirus, which originated in China and quickly spread to other countries. A nationwide lockdown was imposed to reduce the spread of this highly infectious disease. Social distancing became the new norm and isolated people from their friends. The only way to break the monotony was to inveigle an invitation to Jain's home. When Gautam realized they had taken a different route, he was told that the Jains had shifted their residence.

After the initial greetings, both the ladies expressed the increased stress in their lives due to stay-at-home measures and people working from home. Then the men discussed the current pandemic situation.

"Coronavirus is being described as the invisible enemy. The entire world is battling the virus, with doctors and nurses on the frontline."

"Is it fair to compare a pandemic to a war? COVID-19 has triggered one of the worst job crises since the Great Depression. The tourism and travel industry are one of the most affected sectors. Due to fluctuating travel restrictions, each country is having its own regulations, and people are preferring to remain within the safety confines of their homes, the travel industry continues to be in the dumps. We are cutting overhead expenses, marketing, and advertising expenses and wooing the ultra-rich to quarantine in our yachts and hotels."

Alok agreed that the situation was indeed very grim, "Hotels, Restaurants, Theme parks, and Cinemas have been shut down. We are making our venue available for hospital beds and hospital employees. Instead of group activities, people are interested in experiential holidays, where they can follow their passion-reading, writing, or painting in isolation and close to nature. Workcations are becoming quite popular where we provide all the safety precautions, room service, and free wifi at a discounted price."

Gautam could sense the drastic change in their lifestyle, but he did not want to hurt his friend. Reading his thoughts, Pankaj himself clarified, "Due to lockdown, dad's company was bankrupt. We had to sell the cars when we started defaulting on the loans." Gautam tried to cheer him up, "I am sorry. Things will improve as your father is now managing the workcations. But you had an amazing house in a good locality. Why did you vacate that?" Pankaj replied, "With our bank accounts running dry, it was becoming difficult to maintain that villa. So, we rented it out and shifted here."

Pankaj got worried that even his father might be facing financial problems and he was being kept in the dark. So, one day, he asked his father, "Dad, judging by their lifestyle, I always thought that Jains are very rich. But, when we visited them, they appeared to be in a financial mess. Are we also affected due to the pandemic?" His father cleared all his doubts, "We rely on outward appearances like a fancy car, fancy house to gauge financial success as we cannot see other people's savings, retirement plans, or investment portfolios. If your expenses are higher than your income, one day you are going to be broke. Do you know the difference between being wealthy and being rich?"

Innocently, Pankaj replied, "Both imply the same- having lots of money".

His father corrected him, "The two words might seem like synonyms, but they are completely different. Rich people spend their income to live a lavish lifestyle. On the other hand, wealthy people focus on savings to create a sustainable lifestyle. I don't want to be called rich."

Gautam was proud of his father, "Very true. Spending money to show people how much money you have is the fastest way to lose money. Warren Buffet is a frugal millionaire who quoted, "If you start buying things you don't need, one day you shall have to sell things that you need."

Gautam's mother, who had been listening to the father-son conversation, served them hot milk, saying, "Always remember that humility, kindness, and empathy will earn you more respect than money ever will."

Nilesh recollected having read somewhere, "Wealth is measured in time, not in dollars. My prodigal son, I have been investing wisely for the last twenty years and can retire whenever I wish to and follow my passions."

After wishing each other goodnight, the family retired for the night.

Shield And Weapon

It was late evening and Sidharth was troubleshooting a project, which he had to present before the management of the company where he worked. Not a people person, Sid loved coding and the laptop was his inseparable companion. A simple man, he found happiness in solitary activities like reading a book, painting, and going for a walk. Totally of the opposite nature, his wife Shalini who was an event organizer loved people-centric endeavors. Elegant, stylish, and well-groomed, she was easily noticeable in a crowd. She sought pleasure in social activities-high-end kitty parties, vacations abroad, and nightclubs. That evening, she was busy with fun events at a celebrity kid's birthday party. It had taken six weeks of immaculate planning and the parents were very pleased with all the arrangements. As her work took her to distant locations, her concerned husband gifted her a four-wheeler and Ameya was their chauffeur.

Tall and handsome, Ameya had a majestic personality. During their travel time, they frequently indulged in interesting conversations. Chatting with him on daily basis, she realized that they shared many common interests and their friendship blossomed. Sid used to frequently go on official trips and Ameya and Shalini would go for long drives, to clubs and movies. Ameya always practiced etiquette in social gatherings and many times, people mistook him for Shalini's husband. Fully aware that she was a high-maintenance woman, and he was merely a driver, he was dubious of the future of their relationship.

Life with Sid was monotonous and Shalini wanted to escape from the humdrum of his life. So, one day while going back home, she jokingly proposed to him, "Ameya, why don't we get married?" Caught unawares, his heart skipped a beat and he fumbled, "But.. But I am just a driver. Financially, we are miles apart." Sensing his apprehensions, she placed her palm on his hand, " Don't worry, there is a solution for everything." She connived a plan with Ameya, "I will lodge a police complaint against my husband and in-laws for dowry harassment. The laws are in our favor. So, without any verification, cops will arrest my dear husband and his parents and put them behind the bars." Puzzled, Ameya questioned her, "How is that going to help us financially?" She grinned slyly, " Sid's brother, Suresh is a reputed and successful entrepreneur. To save the family's reputation, he will surely come forward for an amicable out-of-court settlement."

After one week, the wicked plan was executed. Shocked and pained, devastated Suresh succumbed to all her sky-rocketing demands. Demonic Shalini walked away with one luxurious apartment and a crore of cash. Sid was deeply anguished by his wife's evil plans and divorced her. Shalini and Ameya moved to a different city, where Shalini continued to work. Ameya used the booty to buy a fleet of cars and start his own taxi service. Life was total bliss, and they lived the good life- exotic vacations, never-ending parties, and nightclubs. Due to the advent of app-based taxi services, the business suffered huge losses and had to be closed. Shalini's work kept her away from home for long hours. Left alone at home, Ameya started drinking heavily and his health deteriorated. He started abusing Shalini, and there was trouble in paradise.

One day, her boss called her, "Shalini, we have to curate an art exhibition and I will be happy if you take charge of the event." She thanked him for giving her the opportunity and started working on it. While editing the invitations, she had butterflies in her stomach after reading the artist's name: Sidharth Akash Kapur. She felt distraught, "Is he the same Sid-her husband?" He loved painting, but only as a pastime and not as a profession. Scared to death of facing him, she went on leave during the dates of the exhibition. Her doubts were confirmed on seeing the inauguration video shared by her friends.

To feed her curiosity, she called her friend Nidhi, "I hope the event went smoothly. Did you meet the artist? " Nidhi sounded deeply impressed by the artist, "Our Sir is very happy with your work. Everything was perfectly organized. The paintings were exquisite masterpieces. I found it so difficult to believe that he was not a professional artist. He is the country head of a leading software company, and he is pursuing painting as a hobby. Shalini googled him and came across his blogs on fitness and yoga. He had sold his paintings in exhibitions across the world at exorbitant prices. He had even published a book, "FOUR NINE EIGHT A".

She came across his interview during the release of his book. Tears welled up in her eyes as she listened to his voice after so many years. The host of the show congratulated him on his book and asked him, "Mr. Sid, could you please share with the audience what led you to write on this topic?" There was turmoil in his voice when he replied, "Our peaceful family life was shattered because of one fault complaint by my ex-wife. To forget the painful past, I immersed myself in my work and hobbies like blogging, painting, and writing books. I want to make the public aware of this legal terrorism against men. So much has been said and written about the atrocities committed on women but sadly nothing on modern man's plight."

The host of the show read a few excerpts from the preface, "Section 498a was designed and inserted into a legal framework to protect women from harassment for dowry demands. In today's world, when both men and women are working and independent, the very concept of marriage has undergone a dramatic shift. Women are taking undue advantage of the law to harass their husbands and in-laws. In more than 95% of the cases, the allegations turn out to be mala-fide. The husband and in-laws may be acquitted, but that does not wipe out the ignominy suffered before and after the trial. Section 498a, which was supposed to act as a shield for helpless women, is being used as a weapon by a modern woman to wreak vengeance on her husband and his family"

Then Sidharth requested women not to misuse the law. He also called upon authorities to take necessary steps to put check on this illegal practice. Otherwise, the genuine call for help by real victims of domestic violence and cruelty will also be looked upon with suspicion and suppressed.

Loneliness And Solitude

Raghuvinder Singh had just returned to his village from Mumbai. Bubbling with excitement, Chintu ran across the house, " Chachu has come, Chachu has come." Chintu was the youngest son of Ravi, his elder brother. Entering, he quickly glanced over the huge haveli. There was a huge courtyard with a pond in the center and all the other spaces were built around it. There was ample sunshine, fresh air, and rain in the house. His grandparents, parents, uncles, and aunts lived together harmoniously. Each family had its own house around the courtyard, and small children played in the common passage connecting all the houses. After meeting his parents, he retired to his room. As he was tired from the journey, he decided to meet the other members of the family in the evening.

While relaxing in his room, he took a good trip down the memory lane to his childhood days and the journey till then. He had a carefree childhood. He enjoyed running in the fields, climbing the trees, playing hide and seek, and taking bath in the water canal. His village was more like a small town with all the modern facilities like good schools and colleges, electricity, water, and internet, but he always wanted to experience city life. He got a job offer in Mumbai after completing his Diploma in Computer Hardware and Maintenance. The entire family came to the station to bid him goodbye. His mother could not hold back her tears. "Raghu, do not travel by local train during peak hours. Beware of pickpockets. Eat properly. "

Once in Mumbai, he was enchanted by the city's magnetic aura, the hustle and bustle, high-rise buildings, malls, metros, local trains, and soul-soothing beaches. His office, a laptop repair center, was on a mezzanine floor, which could be reached by a narrow wooden staircase. He rented a small studio apartment close to his office to avoid the travel woes. His colleagues were warm and friendly. They lived in the distant suburbs and used to commute by local trains. During the lunch break, they would share their experiences of rushing to catch the train, struggling to stand comfortably, and then being pushed out at the destination station.

After a few months, the daily routine of going to work and coming back to an empty flat became monotonous. He did not know his neighbors. There was no one to talk to, no constant dropping in of friends, nothing to relieve the monotony of daily life. The people in the city were too ambitious and engrossed in their race towards fame and success. Back in his village, people knew each other by their names. They were more relaxed and were always ready to spend time with each other. He felt lonely and lost in a city with a maximum density of population. He missed his family while having dinner alone in his apartment. He painfully remembered how the entire family gathered in the hall for dinner, sharing their experiences of the day and cracking jokes. He said to himself, "They too must be missing me."

One Sunday morning, while strolling around the Mumbai streets, he came across a secluded spot. The old wooden gate was open, and he just walked in. He was surprised to see a lush green forest with a temple in the middle. At the entrance was a huge banyan tree, expanding over a large area. He sat on one of the cement benches under the tree, listening to the chirping of a variety of birds. Occasionally, he could hear the grunting of monkeys as they scrambled from one tree to another.

The temple was an old structure, dedicated to Lord Ganesh. After offering his prayers to the elephant deity, he meandered around the small forest. The dense sky-touching trees were blocking the sunlight, and it was very cool. The tranquil atmosphere amid the city's clamor appealed to him. He sighted one hermit sitting peacefully with his eyes closed. There was a certain peace and calmness in his countenance. He was clad in a white dhoti and had a rudraksha mala around his neck. He fell in love with this place, an oasis amid a chaotic city. He felt close to nature and found it rejuvenating and relaxing. He started visiting it regularly. Sometimes, the hermit would acknowledge his presence by nodding his head. Raghu was urged to strike up a conversation with him, but he was unsure if the hermit would entertain him. He reflected, "He lives in the forest all by himself. Doesn't he feel lonely? " One day, he was relaxing under the banyan tree when the hermit came and sat next to him, "Son, I see you coming here regularly. It seems something is disturbing you. " Raghu was astonished, "This hermit speaks English, and that too with an accent!" He briefly talked about himself, his journey to Mumbai, and how much he missed his family.

Next Sunday, he asked him, "Don't you feel lonely here, living all by yourself?" He smiled and said, "I am enjoying this solitude. I enjoy my own company. I am writing a book and I can concentrate here." All this perplexed Raghu even more. "A hermit and a book!", he exclaimed. Every Sunday, he started spending time with him. He was intrigued by his life story. He could not believe that this simple dhoti-clad man was an engineer by profession, had studied and worked in the U.S., and had traveled worldwide. He did not even know his name and addresses him as 'Guruji".

One day Guruji told him the story of his life. "My name is Daya Shankar. I was living the good life in the golden state of California with my wife Sujata and five-year-old daughter Tanya. Both of us were working for the same software firm. My parents frequently visited us and took care of Tanya." During Christmas Vacations, they all decided to visit India so that Tanya would get some exposure to Indian culture and meet her cousins. As his project was nearing completion, he could not join them. He went to see them off at the airport, visited one of his friends, and was driving back home when the phone rang. The aircraft with all his family members on board crashed just five minutes after take-off. In seconds, the aircraft blew up in flames and his entire family-wife, daughter, and parents were completely wiped out.

He continued, "Being the only child, I did not have any shoulder to lean on and share the grief. I was shocked, sad, and lonely in America. Every day going to the office had become an uphill task. Grief-stricken, I started contemplating suicide." One of his Indian friends advised him to join Yoga and meditation Centre. Meditation stabilized his troubled and agitated mind. But loneliness was killing him inside. He read many self-help books on loneliness, listened to audio tapes, and attended workshops but none of them gave any practical solutions to the problems he was facing. That time he resolved to write a book on this topic himself. After doing sufficient research and collecting the required material, he returned to India. He said, "Loneliness is one of the biggest problems in the world. The British Prime-minister has appointed a minister of loneliness, a sad reality of modern life." Raghu pleaded with him to enlighten him on the book but guruji firmly replied, "It is time for my yoga. Next Sunday."

Raghu was restless the whole week. Next Sunday, he briefly introduced him to his book titled, 'Loneliness and Solitude.' Raghu could not understand the difference between the two words and innocently asked, "Both the words have the same meaning -being alone." Daya Shankar explained, "Loneliness is the pain of being alone and Solitude is the glory of being alone. Loneliness is marked by a feeling of isolation. You can be surrounded by people and still feel lonely." He continued, "Solitude is the state of being alone without being lonely, where you provide yourself a wonderful and sufficient company." He then quoted the words of famous inventor Nikola Tesla, " The mind is sharper and keener in seclusion and uninterrupted solitude. Ideas are born when you are alone." His book was written with the purpose to give practical solutions to help people combat loneliness and be blissful in their own company.

Raghu was allured by his wisdom and intellect. He could not decide whether to continue living in Mumbai or go back to his village. Daya Shankar helped him resolve his dilemma. He suggested he should stay in Mumbai for two years and sharpen his skills in laptop repairing and then start his center in his village. Raghu thanked him for his advice. He said, "I am fortunate to be born in an affluent zamindar family. I could afford to rent a house near my office. I have seen people from my village coming to Mumbai in search of work. They travel in cramped trains and gamble with their lives every day to reach the office on time." If he succeeded in his venture, some of them could be employed in the village itself. He also enrolled in weekend courses on economics, financial management, human relationship, and management.

After two years of hard work, having gained the confidence and maturity to work independently, he returned to his village. He found it amusing that the maximum city taught him to fight loneliness and enjoy solitude.

Be Unreasonable

After a long walk in the fields by the riverside, relaxing on a swing and sipping fresh coconut water, Shalini was merrily observing Karan and Khushboo. They would run into the house and emerge with all sorts of discarded material—plastic bottles, containers, cold drink cans, and electronic waste—and pile them neatly in one corner. After ensuring the kids had not left anything behind, their mother came out and told Shalini, "This is a ritual followed by every household each Sunday." Shalini, a marketing executive from Mumbai, was on a brief holiday visiting her sister, whose husband had gone with his parents on a pilgrimage. She enjoyed every moment spent with her sister's young children.

Rajini joined her sister on the swing and the two kids started pushing the swing. Confused, Shalini asked her sister, "Didi, don't you have any garbage collection mechanism like we have in Mumbai?" Rajini replied sarcastically, "Oh, that is why we find garbage littered across Mumbai's streets. It all started with our mission to keep the river clean. At a young age, the importance of a clean environment is emphasized to children. They are taught not to throw anything into the river. Even a single chocolate wrapper should find its way into a bin and not be found lying around." Soon after, two boys in their early twenties came and collected everything in separate gunny bags.

To satisfy Shalini's curiosity, Rajini replied, "The plastic will be reused to make attractive dustbins and pots. We make them in all sizes so that even small children can use them. The kitchen waste is composted and converted to manure. While walking in the lanes, she had seen beautiful, cute dwarf dustbins." Impressed, Shalini could not help admiring the simple procedure followed by the village folks to keep the river and the surroundings clean. The image of Mumbai rivers flashed across her mind-stagnant, black, stanching water, "I was always under the impression that Mithi was a nullah. It was only after the 2005 deluge that I came to know that it was a river flowing into the Arabian Sea.""

With melancholy in her voice, she told her, "Tomorrow I am leaving for Mumbai. I am going to miss my morning walks in the lush green fields and reading by the riverside." Back home, she resolved to bring the lost sweetness to the Mithi river, true to its name. Despite her busy schedule, she collected information on the rivers in Mumbai and the various river revival projects carried out so far. She found the story of the river Thames very inspiring. Once a very polluted river, the Thames is now one of the cleanest rivers in the world. It took six decades to clean the river.

Always a leader and an activist, she started her project by getting the water tested. The results declared the water unfit for any living creature to survive. Industrial effluents and untreated sewage from the slums were the main cause of polluting the river. It came as a big surprise to her that every day Mumbai generates 7000 tons of garbage, a large portion of which is recycled, and the rejected waste made its way to the river. She was determined to stop the Mithi river from being used as a dumping reservoir.

She did not want to sit back and watch but sprang into action immediately. She pitched in a few friends, and armed with gloves and shovels, they handpicked the littered waste-plastic bottles, old clothes, and plastic bags. In the beginning, the slum dwellers, and the passers-by found all this activity weird and gave them strange looks. All that did not deter them. But they were disappointed by the re-appearance of garbage at the same place cleaned by them. She visited municipal corporations and consulted environmentalists and NGOs. Gradually, the group of few girls also grew in number. She arranged street plays urging people to save the largest freshwater bodies. She addressed rallies, "We cannot rely on the government or authorities to take care of the city and the waste generated by us. It is everybody's duty and responsibility to preserve Mother Nature. If we have clean rivers, we will have clean beaches. Whatever enters the river, flows into the sea and then we consume fish which has swallowed microplastic."

There was an exponential rise in the number of volunteers. A petition to save the rivers duly signed by the responsible citizens was submitted to the Chief Minister. Seeing the public interest, a committee was set up which proposed a few steps for cleaning the river.

1. Propel the plans for cleaning the river. For this purpose, underground tunnels were proposed for carrying sewage to sewage treatment plants.

2. Prevent industrial wastage and sewage from entering the river.

3. Fish like Tilapia and Gambusia were released into the river.

4. Educate the people to revere the rivers.

After a few years of endeavor, the Mithi river started showing signs of a rebound, with ecosystems and fisheries coming back. Just like the river in the village, there were riverbanks on both sides along its entire length. Rejuvenated, the Mithi river became a tourist attraction. Children loved the arch bridges, a shoal of fish, and biodiversity on both sides of the river. She was felicitated by her school on their Annual Day. In her address note, she shared her story with the students, "During the initial years, my parents were not very supportive of what I was doing. Even my neighbors and relatives looked upon me as a troublemaker. While holding rallies, I was arrested twice. But I resolved to be unshakable from within and focused only on my goal- A clean, sweet Mithi river." Loud applause followed. She continued, "While distributing pamphlets, I used to be disappointed to see wealthy people zoom past by the river in their limousines, oblivious of the gargantuan issues facing mankind. I strongly believe that it is a sin to be silent when you must protest. This mission could not have been successful without the support of all of you. I take this opportunity to thank all my friends, volunteers, and organizations. I urge all of you to be the people who change time."

In the end, she quoted G B Shaw, "Reasonable man adapts himself to the world; the unreasonable one persists in trying to adapt the world to himself, therefore all the progress depends on the unreasonable man."

Lead The Way

Vinita and her husband, Alok Mehra, were silently driving back home after collecting their son's progress card. For the umpteenth time, Vinita read the remarks on the report card: "Not Satisfactory." Their son, Vinay, had been an exceptionally bright student and was always a topper, but gradually his class rank began sliding down. She said enigmatically, "Vinay is a very industrious and intelligent child who never wastes his time. We should try to investigate the real cause of his poor academic performance before he loses his confidence. Poor child, his goal of becoming a doctor should not remain a faded dream."

Concerned and worried, Vinita took a sabbatical for six months and started coaching Vinay. Visits to academic counselors for guidance proved futile. Despite all this, they put up a brave face and took him out for picnics, science exhibitions, and movies. One evening Vinita invited her colleague Shalini and her husband, Dr. Ashwin for dinner. They all relished the delicious dinner and then went for a stroll. Dr. Ashwin, a child specialist observed that as compared to other kids of his age, Vinay was getting tired and breathless very quickly. His parents then shared their grave concern and helplessness for his falling grades. Dr. Ashwin recommended a few blood tests to be done and prescribed some tonics. Two days later, Alok was quite relieved when he was in receipt of the blood test reports and all the parameters were in the correct range.

Next weekend, Dr. Ashwin invited Vinita and Alok to his clinic. He drew the parents' attention to the traces of lead in the blood sample. Alok replied casually. "Lead concentration is minuscule-5microgram/dL, which is negligible and should not have detrimental effects on health." Dr. Ashwin enlightened them, "Lead inhibits the bodies of growing children from absorbing important minerals like iron, zinc, and Calcium which are essential for brain and nerve development." Shalini asked curiously, "Does Lead play any significant role like other minerals? Can you please tell us about the safe levels of blood lead?" Dr. Ashwin replied calmly, "To date, the safe level of blood lead has not been identified. Lead does not serve any useful purpose in the human body."

Mehras were confused and finding it difficult to believe as their son had never shown symptoms of any kind of poisoning. Dr. Ashwin told them that children who have been exposed to lead usually do not show any symptoms until they are in middle school. The parents were disappointed when they were told that Chelation is the only drug for lead poisoning which unfortunately is not easily available. The best and only solution lies in finding and removing the source of lead to prevent further exposure.

Determined to find the source of Lead in her son's blood, Vinita started reading voraciously about lead poisoning in children. Experts could not find any traces of lead in their environment. The building had been painted recently using lead-free paint. Air, drinking water, and the soil in the ground where they resided were lead-free. The Mehra family owned a farmhouse on the outskirts of the city. When Vinita requested her husband to get the soil and water at the farmhouse tested, he just laughed it away, "We go to the farmhouse to take respite from the pollution of the city. And you want to test pollution levels there also. I think you are reading too many articles on pollution." Vinita remembered the doctor's words, "The only solution is to find the source." Tests were carried out at the farmhouse and the results showed that the soil was heavily contaminated with lead. The fruits and vegetables delivered to their residence were supposed to be organic but could also have been the major cause. Vinita always used to take pride in her 'Direct from farm products' little knowing about the insidious damage being caused by the lead in them.

The lead-based painting on the exterior wall and swings and slides in the playground and the nearby mining industry contributed to the increased level of lead in the soil. Young Vinay might have accidentally swallowed the contaminated soil while playing. Having identified the source, Mehras regained their lost confidence and comforted themselves that they could prevent further damage. Doctors carried out further investigation to fathom the damage caused by lead and the parents were dumbstruck when they were informed about the lead deposition on the teeth and bones resulting in irreversible damage. Vinita gradually accepted the painful condition that could not be changed but felt the urge to increase awareness about this little-known gargantuan issue. Worldwide, millions of children were getting affected by lead poisoning. Developed countries had taken necessary measures and were able to control lead pollution.

In developing countries like India, lead has been found in food items like chili powder, garam masala, cosmetics, and a brand of instant noodles. Vinita worked hard with various NGOs and environmentalists to increase public awareness. She organized street plays and displayed banners across the city urging people not to let children swallow soil and dirt. She also held meetings with politicians and industrialists and made great efforts to accelerate the phasing out of leaded gasoline and paints containing lead.

In one year, the levels of lead pollution declined drastically. Miraculously, by God's grace, Vinay also showed remarkable progress and his grades improved. Vinay felt proud of his mother for all the adulations and awards she received for her incipit contribution for making the environment lead-free.

Think, Don't Judge

Monica, a young lady had loaded her shopping trolley with all the necessary items and was standing in a queue at the billing counter of the supermarket. She looked edgy in a short skirt and sleeveless top. Listening to music on headphones, she kept glancing at her watch restlessly. At the counter, a young boy who seemed to be in his late teens, helped her in putting the things in her shopping bag. She had purchased cold drinks, snacks, disposable plates, and glasses. While handing the bag to her, he gave her a sly grin, as if trying to say, "Have fun. Enjoy the party madam". Uncomfortable with his behavior, Monica grabbed her bag and quickly left the shop.

She had to finalize the menu for the party that evening and had parked her car at the caterer's office. As she was walking toward the car, she had a feeling as if she was being followed by the boy at the counter. She turned around and found the boy walking briskly towards her. Scared, she started marching faster, "I suspected him from the very beginning. The way he was smiling at me.' She took a detour through small lanes, but he did not lose sight of her. Finally, when she was keeping her shopping bag in the car boot, the boy stood in front of her, panting for breath. Before she could say anything, he showed his badge to her and handed her the wallet, which she had forgotten at the counter. Taken by surprise, she could only say, "Thank you."

While going back to the shop, the boy said to himself, "These spoiled children from wealthy families don't have value for anything. They are always in a hurry." Monica regretted having judged the boy wrongly. The badge conveyed that he was a student of 'Dilkhush school', a school for deaf and mute children. She felt indebted to him for returning her wallet which contained her passport, credit cards, and other identity cards. On her next visit to the supermarket, she looked around for the boy. Unable to locate him, she met the shop manager. He informed her, "Once a week, students from Dilkush school visit the market and spend the entire day with them. This exercise is carried out to draw them into community service, which is going to help them in their later lives. Also, it guards them against their loneliness." She briefly told the manager about herself, and he obliged her by sharing personal information about the boy.

After making an appointment, she visited his family. Both his parents were working. His name was Bhavesh, and he had a younger brother, Bhavik. Bhavesh recognized her and it was a pleasant surprise for him to see her. His mother offered her tea and snacks and narrated his story, "We were very happy when he was born. He has always been a very active child and when he was one year old, he was babbling words like, "Mama, Papa" He used to stand on the balcony and wave "Ta-ta Ta-ta" to passers-by. He lost his hearing ability after a bout of meningitis. It was very difficult for us to accept that our child can no longer speak and hear. We ensure that he leads a happy and respectable life." Bhavesh's father added, "It is a silent visual world for him. He is usually happy, but he feels uncomfortable when some people just stare at him as if he is an alien from the outer place. He likes everything bright and shiny."

Bhavick showed his brother's drawing book to her. Monica could not help admiring the beautiful sketches and paintings, "He is very talented, and we should give a proper direction to his imagination and creativity. I will contact the National Deaf Children Society and ask them to assist him in following his passion for drawing." Bhavesh's father had already heard about her, "Beti, you are associated with another organization, "Nari Shakti". Bhavik also showed interest in her association with the NGOs. Using sign language, he was communicating with Bhavesh. He urged, "Didi, please tell us your story."

All of them listened silently as she told them her story. "My mother used to work as a bar dancer. I grew up loathing her profession. Gradually, I learned to appreciate her efforts to earn a living. I had a strong determination not to follow in her footsteps and do something else with my life. Many activists associated with various NGOs used to visit our area and counsel the womenfolk and children. I listened to them attentively, hoping they will help me turn my world around. I was not very academically inclined, and I frequently switched NGOs and schools resulting in breaks in my school education."

One evening, a few volunteers from an NGO asked her if she would like to participate in a street play, scripted to create awareness of the safety of girl children. She happily agreed and they rehearsed regularly before performing in malls all over the city. She was appreciated for her confidence, voice projection, spontaneity, and acting skills. Then she got an opportunity to perform in theatre and she was happy as she was being compensated well. She joined some diction and etiquette classes and was selected for a play to be performed in New York. She was very excited as nobody in their family had gone abroad. She wanted to pursue a course in

Performing Arts from the famous 'New York Fundie Academy'. She pointed out, "Unlike our local colleges which insist on marks, foreign universities pay heed to our background, grit, resilience, and other skills. Luckily, I secured admission with a full scholarship."

She continued, "Back in India, I continue to work with the theatre. I have also grabbed a few roles in regional movies. Now I work with NGOs that work for the welfare of children from marginalized backgrounds. I urge the underprivileged children – 'Don't let your past decide whom you are going to be in the future.' They were all so blown over by her that they could not help admiring her grit and confidence. Before leaving, she asked Bhavik to send her Bhavesh's drawings and testimonials. After she had left, Bhavik communicated everything to his brother using sign language. Bhavesh was dumbfounded. He regretted that he judged her wrongly. Her life was marked by pain and yet she radiated an unusual sense of peace and contentment.

A few weeks later, she called Bhavesh's father, "Congratulations, uncle. Bhavesh will be going to Paris to study Fine Arts. We will raise funds for him through crowdfunding." All of them were very excited and grateful to Monica. Both Monica and Bhavesh had wrongly judged each other. The world of outer appearance is just a façade and shallow.

Carl Jung rightly quoted, "Thinking is difficult, that's why most people judge." We are always judging people, judging things, and judging circumstances. Many times, we judge a person or a situation and later on realize we were completely wrong.

Wealthy And Happy

It was pouring heavily. Sanjay was savoring his hot cup of tea and pakoras in a small, shanty restaurant watching the pelting rain drops. He was working as a driver for the Nair family. His boss and his wife were attending a wedding reception and he was waiting to drive them back home. A blind beggar couple rushed to the stall to take shelter from the rain and squatted outside on the floor. They looked pitiful and repugnant in filthy rags and matty, unkempt hair. Sanjay had frequently seen this couple begging on the local train. The lady held a stick which she used to keep hitting to left and right and the man rested his arms on her shoulder. They would sing religious songs. He remembered them because of their melodious voice. The man had an incredible aura, and his smiling face illuminated the surroundings. People used to give them money and food. In return, they used to bless them, "May God bless you. Whatever you give, comes back to you manifold."

Since he had plenty of time at his disposal, he ordered tea and pakoras for the couple. To quench his curiosity about them, he attempted to initiate a conversation with them. After greeting them, he asked, "Chacha, how are you? Every day, I see you on the local train. You sing very well. Are you not scared of entering the train at one station, exiting and entering a different compartment at the next station?" The blind man replied, "Son, why should we worry when God is taking care of all of us? We are happy together. I am completely blind, but she has partial vision in her right eye. So, she guides me, and I follow her blindly. People have been kind and generous to us. From the money we collect, we buy biscuits and snacks for the small children so that they do not sleep hungry. People help us in crossing the roads We don't own anything, and we don't have the fear of losing anything."

Sanjay was flabbergasted by their joie-de-vivre. He said to himself, "They have not read any self-help books. Without a life coach, they have embraced life and its challenges. Whatever little they have, they are ready to share with the less unfortunate ones." A few months back, his son had to undergo emergency surgery. He had approached his boss for some financial help to be adjusted against his salary. He blatantly refused to help him and even deducted his salary for the few days he could not report for work. It was time for him to drive his boss back home. He gave them a ten rupee note and went to the parking space to take out the car.

On the way back home, the Nair couple sat silently. While Mr. Nair was engrossed in his mobile, the lady kept looking out of the window. They always looked so emotionally cold and detached. The lady was looking elegant in her statement Kanjeevaram saree, heavy pearl earrings, and a stunning emerald choker. Without a smile, her painted face with mascara and dark lipstick did not exude any charm. Mr. Nair scowled and grimaced in his classic business suite. After parking the car, he went to their house to deposit the car keys. The sprawling living room with glass walls from floor to ceiling was decked in grandiose. Mr. Nair took the keys and in a low, chilling voice said, "Tomorrow, come at 8 am."

The next day, he was present at Nair's residence at sharp 8 am. After leaving him at the office, he chatted with the other drivers. They told him the Nair's rags to riches story. One driver said, "Mr. Nair immersed himself in his work to be successful and neglected his personal life. His wife felt lonely and rejected while her husband was toiling day and night. While progressing, they drifted away from their old friends. They made new friends belonging to the so-called 'Higher Class', but they found them shallow and too materialistic. The family was rotting from within due to a lack of meaningful, heartfelt bonding. Their only son was studying in the US. Sanjay reflected, "They should be rejoicing in their success. But it seems the hardships and the struggle squeezed the joy out of their life."

While going back home, he could not help comparing the two couples. The poor, blind couple had a warm understanding between them. They were tolerant, easy-going, and battling their way together with exemplary courage. The man's loud and uncanny laughter was captivating. When the family had gathered for dinner, he shared his feelings with his family. His wife Sanjana was a wise woman and looked after their two sons. Ajay was ten-year-old, and Vijay was looking forward to his sixth birthday. Sanjana said, "We are all born happy. With limited exposure to the outside world, their souls are uncorrupted and pure." Sanjay agreed, "That is the reason behind their childlike innocence. They are happy with whatever little they have, and they have the generosity to share with the young, unfortunate children."

Ajay, "Mr. Nair has all the material comforts money can buy. Can't they transform their money which is in the form of currency into happiness?"

Sanjay, "I have never seen them exchanging pleasantries. They are not celebrating their success. In my eyes, my boss is poor because money is the only thing he possesses.".

Vijay had been listening to all this talk silently. Innocently, he asked, "Papa, you only keep asking us to study hard so that we can get good jobs."

Sanjay took his younger son in his lap and replied, "Money is not evil. Greed is bad. There is nothing wrong in possessing money, but money should not possess you."

Ajay added, "In our moral science class, we were taught that one should earn well and fulfill all his needs. Along with that, you should also utilize your money to serve others."

Sanjana came up with a wonderful suggestion, "This Saturday is Vijay's birthday. We can do something for the beggar couple." All the family members liked the suggestion. So, they approached the beggar couple, "Chacha, you don't have to beg in trains anymore. I have brought one weighing machine for you. Passengers will use this machine and give you money in return." The young children, whom they were supporting also volunteered to help. Ajay had prepared a board on which he had written:

> **May You Have A Beautiful Day**
> **I Cannot See**
> **I Can Only Pray For You**

People donated generously. Slowly, they started selling combs, handkerchiefs, etc.

Sanjay was happy that his sons understood the value of happiness and money. True wealth and happiness are not measured by material possessions. True wealth is determined by the things you possess that money cannot buy -inner fulfillment, joy, unconditional love, peace, and contentment.

Contribution And Competition

It was the month of May, summer vacation for school children. In one of the bungalows in South Delhi, a brother-sister duo was playing chess. After serving them sweet lassi, their mother told them, "Karan and Khushi, don't venture out in the hot sun to pluck mangoes." She then went to take a short nap. Karan loved his younger sister Khushi. Although only two years older, he was very protective of her. He was truly her 'Big Brother'. Karan was in the tenth standard and studying hard for his board exams. Khushi was studying in the eighth standard in the same school. While playing chess, Karan would deliberately make some wrong moves to let his kid sister win and her victory smile brought him joy. She would run around the house, jumping and clapping, "I won. I won." The house resounded with her laughter. Not only chess, but Karan also always allowed his sister to win whatever game they played -carrom-board, badminton, or a simple bicycle race.

Khushi was a winner not only at home but at school also. Apart from academics and sports, she also excelled in elocution, essay writing, and poetry. A consistent winner, the trophies and medals won by her were proudly displayed in her room in a glass cabinet. When she went to school after vacation, one banner caught her attention. St. Mary's school was organizing an event where eminent psychologists and social activists would discuss the problems faced by a girl child in India. Essays were invited from students concerning this topic. Khushi drafted the essay which was later edited by her mother. A few weeks later, her school principal called her and two more students from different sections, "Congratulations, I am happy that you will be representing our school for the event. All the best." Khushi told her mother about the upcoming event. Since she was busy with her exams and could not devote much time to the event, her mother helped her by collecting a few related articles from the magazines.

Her father dropped her at St. Mary's school for the event. She was feeling a bit uneasy as she had been busy with her examinations and was not well-prepared. Her father told her, "Relax. Do your best." After registration, volunteers directed her to the seminar hall. The hall was nearly full, bubbling with enthusiasm. School children always find it exciting to attend events hosted by other schools. For intra-school events, there was a certain uniform pattern in the audience as they were all attired in the school uniform of a white shirt and blue skirt. But here the hall was very colorful and vibrant with so many children from different schools in their respective uniforms. Khushi searched for her schoolmates and joined them.

The event started with a Welcome speech by the school Principal. Then the coordinator explained the day's program. They would be shown a few short films showing the plight of girls across India, which would be followed by discussions on the various characters portrayed in the film. The first short film was about the story of a young bright girl named Lata. Her father was a drunkard and her mother used to work in the fields. They lived in a remote village and the nearest school was 10 Kms. away. Lata had to drop out of school, but her younger brother, Bharat continued his schooling. After coming from school, he played the whole day and studied in the evening. Lata had to cook for the family, clean the utensils, wash the clothes, and do all other household chores. Her father only cursed her and beat her. "Why I was born as a girl in this house?", she would cry to herself.

Like this, they were shown many documentary films on child marriages, girl trafficking, and the education of girl-child. At the end of each film, lights were put on. Two teachers came on the stage and interacted with the students. They discussed the miserable plight of girls in rural India and how to change the attitude of the public towards them. All of them felt that the girls should be taught some skills which will make them capable of earning their livelihood and leading respectable and independent lives. Khushi felt blessed, "My parents send me to one of the best schools in the city. They encourage me to be successful in life. Karan is so protective and caring." To maintain decorum, students had to raise their hands whenever they wished to say something. The volunteers would pass the microphone to them. Khushi participated actively. She carefully listened to the opinion of other students. She was blown away by the deliverance, confidence, and vocabulary of the girls from other schools. In the closing ceremony, the social activist summarized the important points discussed. Even though she mentioned her name along with a few students who had participated actively, Khushi felt unhappy. She felt she could have delivered better and given tough competition to the other girls. She regretted, "Immediately after the exams got over, I should have browsed through the articles mom had collected."

After the event, she went home with her father. He could sense that she was not her jolly self and they drove home silently. Entering the home, she wailed, "Everyone's comments were better than mine." Karan retorted, "Why are you always competing with others? Anyway, it was not a competition but an event for a noble cause." At the dinner table, everyone was silent. When Khushi, the joy of the house is not happy, other members could not be happy. Her father was concerned about this 'winner attitude' of Khushi. He did not want to discourage her. He was concerned that her daughter had limited exposure. Till then, she had been competing mostly at events in her school. She should be able to handle failures also. After dinner, her father said, "Khushi, you did your best in today's event. You were even appreciated for your valuable contributions. Let me enlighten you on an especially important life lesson. Always Contribute. Never Compete. Contribution is better than competing."

While their mother was clearing the table, both the children listened to their father attentively. He continued, "As individuals, we are always trying to undo each other in every sphere of life. All of us are endowed with unlimited potential and we should unleash it by contributing to society. By competing with others, we are limiting our potential." Khushi interrupted "But daddy, competition is a good thing. It forces us to do our best. It keeps us on our toes and ensures that we never get complacent." Her father agreed but emphasized, "You will face competition at every phase of your life. The ultimate victory in competition is derived from the inner satisfaction of knowing that you have done your best. Every individual is unique and has his gifts. Be unique. Be memorable." He continued, "For a happy, peaceful life we must balance our personal life, professional life, and spiritual life."

Khushi was enthralled by her father's advice and started working on it. In any situation, she would say to herself, "How can I contribute to the best of my ability?" Now, she did not feel jealous of the achievements of other students. She would go out of her way to congratulate them. Being the school captain, she was already a popular figure in the school. She could use her privileged position to make some positive contributions. She took the initiative to plant trees, thereby promoting awareness about the environment.

She started her own "Happy Club". Two students from each class were selected as representatives and they met every day for ten minutes before the school started. If any student needed help of any kind, together they tried to do something. If some student was not well and could not attend school, they helped him with the class notes and assignments. In cities, with mostly nuclear families and both parents working, sometimes students encounter difficult situations at home. Now, they had their club in the school to help them. The club members would collect motivational quotes to be displayed on the noticeboard. Due to all these activities, a strong bonding developed among the students from different classes. They even initiated a compost -bin for the school garden, to compost leftover food from the cafeteria. She continued to excel in academics and extra-curricular activities, but she was not a competitor anymore. She realized that the happiness she derived from serving others was far greater than what her medals and accolades fetched her.

She continued to be actively involved in community work in her college. She started one NGO to provide food and shelter for old and abandoned people. She actively participated in cleanliness drives outside railway stations, bus stands, and other public places. Because of her efforts, people started cleaning up their dog's poo when they were taken for morning walks. Attractive dustbins, in the shape of penguins were placed in the complex so there was no littering of empty containers and other waste. All these activities honed her interpersonal and organizational skills. By doing community service, she became more conscious of her responsibilities towards her family, society, and country.

After graduation, she along with a couple of friends started her own company. She always wanted her products to be easily affordable and useful to mankind. In her own home, her mother used to be irritated by the frequent questions of the maid, "Madam, should the empty cola bottles go along with the dry waste? Madam, in which bin should I throw the wrappers?" This was the story of every household. To explain the classification of dry waste and wet waste to the maids was an onerous task. All this motivated her to collect information on Automatic Waste Segregator and she realized that the available models were expensive and bulky. She wanted to make something compact and easily affordable for everyone. Karan had completed his engineering course and helped her in designing one model. Her father fully supported her in all her ventures. He allowed her to use their outhouse as a workshop. She hired two engineers and a few diploma holders.

The prototype was ready. Since this was her first product, she wanted it to be flawless. She felt that the model could still be improved. She knew that her employees had ideas that had been suppressed and not surfaced. Even though they belonged to the same age group, and she had always been friendly with them, they were not open in their conversations with her. She was getting restless about her product. She remembered her family dinners when they discussed so many things. She started taking her team members for lunch, coffee breaks, and movies. Sometimes, they would all go together or sometimes just two or three employees. After one or two meetings, she got to know them personally and they felt comfortable in her presence. Some of them gave her incredibly good ideas for improving the product and reducing the costs.

Finally, the product was ready. Her team was strong technically but lacked the skills required for marketing. She accompanied them for demonstrating the machine. It was a boon for the housewives. Orders started pouring in. She was finding it difficult to meet the targets. She rented a gala in the industrial area and expanded her team. She started getting orders from all over the country. During her journey, her concern was to serve society and she worked diligently towards it. She was not competing with other start-ups. Many of her friends had gone abroad for higher studies and some of them pursued their management studies in India. She was very content and happy with her achievements. She always remembered her father's words, "Contribute, don't compete" which was the mantra for her success.

Legacy And Legitimacy

Dharmik was sitting in an inclining chair on the verandah of his bungalow. He had just taken out his guitar which was languishing in his cupboard for past so many years. His fingers were bent with rheumatoid arthritis, and he could barely move his stiff fingers over the strings of his guitar. Alone in the palatial house, he revisited his childhood days and his obsession with this musical instrument. He had lost his wife to cancer a few years ago. He eagerly looked forward to his daughter Jaya's annual visit during vacations, with her two school-going children. The house would spring back to life with his daughter's chatter and children scurrying around. Her brother Ajay lived in the same city.

While young, Dharmik faced poverty, hunger, and discrimination. They lived in a chawl, and his parents did menial jobs, but they always prayed for a bright future for their two sons. They worked hard to give them a good education. Their mother would always tell them, "Study hard. Education is the ticket to a good life." Since they did not have any distractions like television, shopping, or parties, they had plenty of time to study. Both the brothers enjoyed studying, solving problems, and proudly showing the report card to their parents. With little exposure to the outside life, reading books, memorizing, and reproducing the same in the examinations had become mechanical and monotonous for Dharmik. He wanted to do something more thrilling and exciting. One day, he came across an old, abandoned guitar. He picked it up, removed the dust with a piece of cloth, and started playing. Playing guitar gave him a kind of pleasure that he had never experienced before. "I wish I could get formal training, rehearse well and perform on stage," he said to himself.

In the evening, after completing his studies, he would relax by playing his guitar. The soft music was soothing to the people who had returned home after a day's hard work. He imagined himself performing on stage with the audience cheering, but he knew very well that it would remain a dream. He made a few futile attempts to convince his parents to allow him to follow his passion and become a guitarist. But they insisted, "Education alone will help all of us in changing our present circumstances." Dejected, he studied hard and was granted a scholarship to pursue his Master of Science. In the hostel, coming from a different background, he had difficulty mingling with other students. After completing his studies, he joined a research institute as a scientist.

He efficiently juggled his time between research work and administrative work. He devoted all his time and energy to building his legitimacy...research papers in renowned international journals, chairing conferences, and discharging all the administrative responsibilities diligently. He was bestowed with many awards and honors for his contribution to science and was appointed the director of the institute. Coming from a humble background, he was parsimonious and wanted to ensure financial security for his family. He purchased a huge house in a good locality. Education loans, home loans, and giving good education to his children remained his priority.

His son Ajay always wanted to become a writer. His plays, stories, and articles received considerable acclaim. He wanted to study English literature, but his father wanted him to become an engineer, "Writing cannot be a full-time profession. You can hone your writing skills along with your studies." However, Ajay was least interested in studies, and he used to bunk classes to watch movies and plays. Whenever a book was being released, he would rush there. He had a burning desire to see his book released one day. And this desire was backed by his strong faith in himself. On one such occasion, he met Vandana, also a young, budding author. They started spending a lot of time together. She encouraged him to follow his passion. While watching movies, he would be intrigued by the story, the lyrics, and the dialogues. He wondered, "How many times these lines must have been written, twisted, and rewritten before the dialogue was finally included in the script? And how many times, the hero must have delivered the same dialogue for the director's satisfaction?" He resolved to himself, "One day, I will also write a script for a movie."

His father was concerned and worried about his obsession with becoming a writer and neglecting his studies which led to frequent arguments in the house. Ajay wanted a tranquil atmosphere to focus on his writing. One day, he left the home, started living with Vandana, and eventually married her. As Vandana had already written a few books, she introduced Ajay to her publishers. Ajay started writing articles for newspapers and magazines and money started pouring in. Secretly,

Dharmik was proud of his son's success. He admired his courage to follow his passion and live his dream. His dream of becoming a guitarist got crushed by poverty.

Entire life, Dharmik focused on building his legitimacy, striving for success and achievement. Sitting alone on the balcony, he regretted not spending enough time with his children. His life revolved only around his research work. Time flies. Now his children had grown up, left the nest, and had their own families. His son always longed for his love. He should have been his pillar of strength and encouraged him to follow his passion.

With due course of time, Ajay soared in popularity. Along with Vandana, he authored some of the best-sellers of their time. It is said that the universe is truly kind. Whatever you wish and dream and pursue it with full devotion, the universe will manifest it for you. One day, he got a call from one of the movie directors, "Hello Ajay, we would like to make a movie based on your novel - The Lonely Girl". Ajay couldn't believe his ears. The director felt that nobody understood the characters portrayed in the book better than him and requested him to write the script.

The movie was a great success. He became a star overnight. His interviews appeared everywhere –television, newspapers, and magazines. He had his own beautiful home in a posh area with all the material comforts. He won several awards for his books. He was happy and content with his achievements. Confucius rightly said, "Choose a job you love, and you will never have to work a day in your life." Following his passion, he never ran out of motivation and inspiration. He was basking in the glory of his success.

Ajay and Vandana were busy with their own lives. They requested him to live with them, but he felt comfortable in his own house. Dharmik had spent his entire life acquiring the huge house and a fat bank balance. Today they held no meaning for him. He said to himself, "My children don't need the house or the money. I should have had faith in my son that he will carve his path to success. The legacy I should have left for my children is not this house or money. It is the time, fond memories, love, and compassion, we should have shared." He went to the research institute and bequeathed his house and all other assets to the institute.

The legacy we leave for our children is not counted in terms of material possessions but memories of a happy childhood.

Ambition, Fame, And Success

Ashok Bansal was relaxing on the lavish beige-colored sofa set. He had just returned home after a hectic day at work. He lived in a plush apartment at Churchgate with his beautiful wife Kamla and daughter, Payal. Ramu, their faithful servant served him tea and snacks. Kamla came into the hall with a worried expression on her face, "Payal has not returned home till now. You are spoiling her. She does not listen to me." Ashok smiled and asked her to relax, "Payal is a very smart and intelligent girl. One day, she will conquer the world and make us proud. Why do you want to cut her wings?"

Ashok and Kamla adored their only child. Kamla was orthodox and Ashok was a non-conformist. Hailing from a typical orthodox Marwari family, Ashok had seen his mother, sisters, and wife leading a very sheltered and domesticated life. He had an entirely different vision for his daughter. He had seen ambitious women in his company climb the corporate ladder and he visualized his daughter being one of them. He would always shield Payal from annoying, interfering relatives who were only interested in getting her married. He always encouraged her to believe in herself, follow her dreams and grab the world by the lapels.

After graduating in commerce, Payal cracked the coveted CAT exam and secured admission to IIM, Calcutta. Her father's joy knew no bounds, but old-fashioned Kamla had her fears, "She should settle down in life. We should start looking for a suitable match for her." Ashok threw a lavish party for his colleagues, friends, and relatives. The family headed to the Maldives for a small vacation. They stayed at an overwater villa and enjoyed island hopping, water sports, and a snorkeling safari. The calm and soothing waves were very relaxing. Thoroughly relaxed and rejuvenated she joined IIMC.

At IIM, she had the opportunity to meet people from diverse backgrounds. Along with academics, she was actively involved in inter-B school competitions, festivals, committee work, internships, and several other activities. All this kept her busy but still, she missed her parents and longed to visit them. So, when JBIM, Mumbai was hosting a Quiz competition, she grabbed the opportunity. Payal said to herself, "The college is close to my house. Along with the quiz, I can spend some good quality time with my parents." The convener of the event, Abhay was from Calcutta, and they became good friends. After the event also, they remained in touch. Payal told him about good restaurants in Mumbai and Abhay told her about Calcutta. Payal was impressed by his views on the education and empowerment of women.

Both got placed in Goldman Sachs, Singapore, and got married before leaving India. Payal was working in the distressed debt department and Abhay was a venture capitalist. Abhay was involved with companies that had just incubated or grown up. On the contrary, Payal was involved with companies that had defaulted or were in financial distress. Abhay would often tease her, "Your company is like a vulture. You survive on dead businesses." Both of them worked hard and were highly successful in their respective careers. Payal was exceptionally good in her analysis and dealing with lawyers and after a few years, she launched her firm. They welcomed their son Abhijeet. So, she had to look after two babies- her company and her son.

Meanwhile, her mother was diagnosed with Alzheimer's disease and her father was looking after her. Abhay was proud of his highly successful wife, but he did not share any responsibility in caregiving. Payal was shocked, surprised, and hurt by this behavior. She always expected an egalitarian marriage, where both of them would support and help each other. Abhay immersed himself in his work. Payal had to manage her job, home, and baby single-handedly. Payal's business was soaring, but her marriage was falling apart. There was nothing left in the marriage, and they were living like roommates. All this affected Abhijeet adversely. Emotionally neglected, he became withdrawn and silent. Even when his parents were at home, they would be working on their laptops or mobile phones. Abhay started feeling miserable and suffocated in this relationship. He moved out of the house and started living with his colleague named Reena. Reena was a divorcee and was living alone. Eventually, Abhay divorced Payal and married Reena.

One day, her father suffered a massive heart attack and passed away. She rushed to India. She was shocked to see her mother in an advanced stage of Alzheimer's, and it deeply pained her when she could not recognize her own daughter. She was hooked to an IV pole and a tube in one nostril to suck out fluid from her stomach. Her father had never given her any inkling about her deteriorating condition as he wanted her to remain focused on her work. Whenever she had enquired about her mother, he would always say, "She is fine. Just becoming forgetful. Sleeps the full day." She resolved to herself, "Papa had full faith in me, and I cannot let him down." She got her mother admitted to a private Nursing home, came back to Singapore, and started working with increased gumption and unbridled enthusiasm,

She entrusted the responsibility of her son and house to her domestic staff. She dedicated all her time and energy to building a business and traveled across the globe. She was juggling so many activities -Branding, marketing, client acquisitions, human resource management, operations, and financial management. She always felt her father was watching her and she was living his dream. She featured among the topmost 50 influential persons in the world and frequently appeared on the front cover of several magazines. Abhijeet saw her mother giving interviews on television, but he sadly reflected, "She never had time for me." He longed for his parents' love and compassion and gradually slipped into depression. His grades were falling. He found comfort in food and had become obese.

One day, she was on a business tour, and she got a call from one of her staff members at home, "Madam, there is an emergency. Please rush back immediately." Her heart skipped a beat. Worried, she called her son but there was no response. An emergency call to the clinic told her that her mother continued to be in the same condition. She rushed back home. Her assistant was at the airport and instead of taking her home, he instructed the driver to take them to Asha hospital. He explained the recent development of events to her in a calm and composed way, "Abhijeet attempted suicide by jumping off the French window of the apartment. Now he is out of danger." Without giving it a second thought, she called Abhay and apprised him of the situation.

It pained her to see Abhijeet. He had suffered multiple fractures and internal injuries. But the real blow came to her when she was told that her son had been taking drugs. Abhay paid a flying visit to the hospital. Nobody made any efforts to understand Abhijeet. Doctors could see the external and internal injuries on his body and treat them. But what about the wounds on his soul? He was an emotionally neglected child and there is no medical equipment to reveal this.

Payal was physically and mentally exhausted. Doctors advised her to go home and take some rest. Sitting alone, she asked herself, "I have always been highly ambitious and achieved fame, success, and recognition for my work. But did I succeed in life? Today, I am ready to do anything to bring my son back home and nurse him." Her empire, which she had struggled to build held no value for her.

Indulgence And Prudence

It was ten- past eight in the morning. Professor Abhay was teaching Engineering Mechanics to Second Year Electrical engineering students. He was a professor of great repute - small, frail, and bespectacled. Students never missed any of his lectures. Mechanics being a mechanical engineering subject, electrical students usually find it onerous. However, Prof. Abhay had his own unique and simple approach to solving complicated problems and that made him popular among students. All the students were engrossed in solving problems. Suddenly, there was a knock at the door. It was Arya. As usual, she was late by ten minutes. Tall and fair, dressed in a black T-shirt and black jeans, she looked devastatingly beautiful.

Prof. Abhay nodded to Arya, signaling her to enter the class. The classroom was fully occupied and there was only one vacant seat on the last bench, next to Rishab. Tall and handsome, Rishabh looked majestic in a white T-shirt and blue jeans. In a hushed tone, Arya asked Rishab to let her write the problem statement and he happily obliged. The following lecture was canceled as Prof. Kalra, who was teaching them Circuit Theory was busy attending an International Conference. Arya requested Rishab to give her company in the canteen, "I was getting late in the morning, and I missed my breakfast." So, Rishab and Arya went to the college canteen for snacks.

Arya was a vivacious girl, bubbling with energy and totally in love with herself. They hit it off immediately. While their classmates were attending classes, very often they could be spotted hanging out at the college canteen. Both of them hailed from affluent families and were not interested in academics as they would be joining the family business.

Arya was staying in the girl's hostel and every day she cycled her way to college. One morning, she had just reached the college when it started pouring heavily. As usual, she was getting late and started pedaling at full speed. She failed to see a pothole, her bicycle skidded, and she fell into a pool of muddy water. She was covered with mud from head to foot. Seeing her condition, her classmate Nandini offered her help, "I live nearby only. You can come with me." Nandini's mother welcomed her with a cup of hot coffee. Nandini was a very sincere and hardworking student. She was liked by all the teachers and students for her simplicity and humility. Whenever Arya felt homesick, she would go to Nandini's home. Nandini also helped Arya with the class assignments.

In the Third year, they went to Nanital on an educational tour. They enjoyed boating in the eye shaped Naini lake. Morning walks around the lake with sun rays pouring through the clouds were rejuvenating. They visited Naina Devi and other places of interest. After dinner, they used to stroll on the famous mall road soaking in the cool breeze from the lake. On the last day of the trip, Rishab proposed to Arya, and she gladly accepted. In the night, when the girls retired to their rooms, Arya broke the news to them. The girls giggled with excitement. Nandini congratulated her, "Undoubtedly, Rishab is a good boy, but he has not been able to secure a job.

He is not career oriented." Arya retorted, "He will be joining his dad's business. The salaries are way too less than the profits in business." Nandini took a minute to think and said slowly, "I feel he should go for a job. Learn discipline, time management, and the art of handling employees, and then go back to business. You will find peace, fulfillment, and a sense of achievement if both of you can take the business to a higher level." Discussions continued and they went to sleep afterward.

Immediately after graduation, Arya and Rishab had the traditional big fat Indian wedding. They vacationed in Europe for a month. Meanwhile, Nandini went to Delhi to pursue her master's from IIT. Rishab and Arya continued to live the good life drenched in opulence. They did not show any inclination towards the business. Their honeymoon continued forever. They visited exotic places all over the world and threw high-profile parties for their friends. A few years later, they were blessed with twins, Abha and Anya. Rishabh's father was growing old. It pained him to see the irresponsible behavior of his son. He just hoped, "Now he has become a father to two daughters. Slowly, he will share the responsibility of running the business." But Rishabh was just not growing up. Never-ending parties, exotic food, and lack of exercise were taking a toll on his health.

Nandini was on the verge of completing her Masters. One evening, she was performing some experiments required for her thesis and suddenly lights went off. The light from the tube light in the corridor shone against the laboratory door. She went and opened the door. Her batchmate Hari was passing by. He asked, "No lights. Can I help you?" "Yes, please come Hari. I am so glad you are here." They had already worked together on mini projects and assignments. He was from a small village in Andhra Pradesh. He had all the qualities Nandini always admired- intelligent, hardworking, and humble. They chatted till lights were restored and developed a good bonding that strengthened with time. Both got placed in top IT companies, got married, and moved to Mumbai. Both worked hard and climbed the corporate ladder. Their son Gautam was a child prodigy. Nandini ensured that their luxurious lifestyle did not spoil him. Nandini was actively involved in various schemes for women and child development. Through their actions, they taught him values such as kindness, self-discipline, and social responsibility. Gautam graduated from IIT and started his own IT company. Business flourished and they had branches across the world.

After his father passed away, Rishabh started looking after the business. He partnered with the wrong people and tried to expand the business. Lack of planning, leadership, and marketing caused the company to fail, and they went deep into debt. Arya remembered Nandini's advice of getting exposure to the corporate world before joining the business. They sold everything and moved to Mumbai along with their daughters. While trying to trace their old friends on social media, Arya contacted Nandini. Nandini felt sorry for them and promised to help them. They accommodated them in one of their flats and the daughters joined Gautam's firm.

Arya felt deeply indebted to Nandini. She had always been helpful, both in college and many years after. Rishabh observed, "Nandini and Hari are highly successful, but they are so modest and humble. Their son, Gautam is so compassionate, responsible, organized, and innovative. I just wasted my time." Arya tried to cheer him, "Forget the past but remember the lessons." They also started working in Mumbai.

It doesn't matter where you come from. By dint of hard work and dedication, one can always improve one's conditions. In life, nothing stays the same forever. You have to keep moving. Heraclitus quoted, "The only constant thing is change. Life is a flux. All things come into being through opposition and all are in flux like a river. Without strife, we cannot grow."

Visible And Invisible

Tension writ large on his face, Mr. Murthy was pacing up and down in his room, frequently glancing at his watch. As the president of a popular cricket league, he had called an emergency meeting of the board members. His assistant called him when all the members had assembled in the seminar hall. After requesting him to arrange tea and snacks, he left for the meeting. He greeted the board members, "Good evening, everyone. I am grateful to all of you for making it convenient to attend today's meeting despite your busy schedules." Waving that day's newspaper in his hands, he continued, "I am sure all of you have read about this unpleasant incident which has become viral and spreading like wildfire. Let us observe the video coverage." So, the lights were put off and the members silently watched the action replay.

The camera had captured two young players, Vikas and Akshaya hurling abuses at each other. The fight took an ugly turn, and the exchange of words was followed by the exchange of blows. They started knocking each other like two boxers. Security guards and a few players rushed to the spot and tried to pacify them. As Akshaya was bleeding from the nose, he was given medical aid and advised to take some rest. The captain requested Vikas to retire to the pavilion. Fuming with anger, he kicked the stumps before leaving.

There was complete silence when the lights were put on. Mr. Murthy shared his apprehensions, "The boys are in the news for the wrong reasons. The media is giving unwarranted publicity to this brawl without mentioning any of the boys' achievements. Next year, they will be playing for the world cup, and I am worried about this kind of misbehavior, which can lead to their suspension." Mr. John, a senior board member completely agreed with the president, "This was certainly not a sight for the world to watch. It is of paramount importance that the players conduct themselves with dignity both on and off the playground." Then he asked the coach, Mr. Rony, to tell them what could have led to this scuffle. Mr. Rony was not aware of any incident which could have triggered the fight, but he asserted that the boys were usually well-behaved and indispensable. This was one of the rare instances when the emotions got the better of them.

In a lighter vein, one member suggested, "All they need is some lessons in moral science." Another member drew their attention to the hectic calendars, "The number of matches being played has increased manifold and the cricketers are bearing the brunt of the stress." The president defended, "We provide them with world-class facilities, excellent coaching, and training facilities and also provide them with proper career opportunities. Still, we are open to suggestions." The coach thanked the board for all the facilities, "Sir, the boys work very hard. All the eleven players in the team have different personalities-some get aggressive while others can remain calm and composed in the same situation. Cricket is not just a bat and ball game played on the field. Not visible, but cricket is played in the head where all the strategic decisions are taken. Apart from the physical fitness, we need players with great mental strength who can deliver consistently for a long period." He then read out the quote by

Jonty Rhodes which was inscribed on one of the walls, "I am convinced things will go much better if the players smile and have some fun on the field, rather than acting like wound-up spring."

Everybody agreed with him that, though underrated -mental strength, focus, and mindset are crucial for every sportsperson to excel in his game. It was unanimously decided to add meditation, yoga, and recreational activities to the daily regimen of cricketers. They would arrange mental health seminars for the players. Mr. Naveen, the team psychologist told them that Amit was dealing with mental health issues and will keep himself away from cricket for a while. An all-rounder, he sounded upset as he could not be there for his mother when she was battling cancer. Now, his wife is expecting their first child and he wants to be there with her. As his coach, he counseled him, and asked him to stay strong and positive, but he burst out crying, "I want to go back home. I miss my family. Hotel rooms are lonely and living out of suitcases is taking a toll on my mental health."

The coach shared his concern for another player, Varun. "He is the youngest player to play test cricket. He is an exciting prodigy with a lot of potentials. Just seventeen he is too young and raw to be in the media glare. He has accumulated a large fan base, especially among teenagers. Many food companies have collaborated with him to endorse their products to increase sales and brand value." Mr. Murthy nodded his head, "Yes, he is seen in commercials for energy drinks, pizzas, and chips. Even my grandson is a huge fan of him and wants to meet him." Mr. Rony narrated an interesting episode, "One day, during a fan meet, the mother of a ten-year-old admonished him in public -My son is a die-hard fan of your game. He insists on having only the products you endorse and imitates your style. It has become a backbreaking job to make him eat healthy food." Varun felt sorry but failed to understand the negative repercussions of his endorsements on adolescents.

Viewed from afar it appears that cricketers lead very exciting lives- chasing fame and money. Many young people are attracted to this profession by the lure of money - staying in five-star hotels, flying business class, and fan following. The anxieties they encounter on daily basis are not seen by other people. Every match played is like taking an examination with the whole world watching. Even the best players have anxiety bouts and sleepless nights before a game. Usually, the fans cheer for their favorite teams to improve their confidence, but they also jeer or boo the opposing team The fan brawl affects the players adversely, brings down their morale, and harms their mental health.

The invisible mental health plays a major role in the performance of the players. All the players must work hard to hone the mental skills needed to keep their minds on the game while playing. It takes a strong mind to predict the game and take decisions instantly.

Pleasure And Happiness

Six-year-old Anil pushed the bowl with his hands and ran away, "I don't want chocos. I want pizza." Lata bai followed her little master from one room to another with the bowl in her hand pleading with him to have his evening snack. He had just returned from school and amid all chaos, his mother called to check if he had returned home safely. He screamed on the phone, "I want to eat pizza" and handed over the phone to Latabai. His mother Alka, who was working as a marketing executive told the maid, "I have a very important meeting with my client. Let the child have whatever he wants."

After savoring the pizza, he played some video games and watched his favorite cartoon serials. Then Lata took him for tuition classes. His mother Alka would fetch him home from classes. Sometimes, she would chit-chat with his teacher and enquire about him. Anil ran to his mother and rummaged through her handbag. A smile lit up his face when his tiny fingers stumbled upon a chocolate bar. On the way back home, his mother asked him about his school and friends.

Anil's father Nilesh was a businessman and usually came home late. When the family sat down for dinner, Lata served them tomato soup. Anil sat with downcast eyes, not daring to look at his parents. His mother chided him, "The soup is getting cold. Should I feed you?" Holding back his tears, Anil said in a meek voice, "I want Chinese." Dog-tired after a hectic day in the office, she was not left with any energy or patience to cajole him to eat the freshly cooked dinner. So, she requested the maid to quickly cook some instant noodles for the brat.

Alka was concerned about her son's addiction to junk food. He was eating only for pleasure and was too young to understand the negative aspects. Due to the addictive taste of fast food, he was not savoring simple home-cooked meals. She tried her best to inculcate healthy food habits in him. She made several unsuccessful attempts to replace chips, French fries, noodles, pizza, and pasta with fruits, salads, and roasted snacks. During the Parent-Teacher Association meeting, his class teacher informed her, "Anil is not attentive in the class. He does not take part in sports or other activities. Otherwise, he is very friendly and gets along well with other children." Without doing any root cause analysis, Alka reduced his playtime and extended the duration of tuition classes by one hour.

With time, chubby-faced roly-poly Anil grew up to be a rotund and paunchy young man. Junk food was ruining his health insidiously, but he continued to hog on the pleasure food. He did not perform well in the competitive examinations and failed to secure admission to reputed colleges in the city. As it was predestined that he would be joining the family business, his parents simply wanted him to have a primary degree from a B-school. After paying huge fees, they enrolled him in a BBA course in a well-known B-school in the city outskirts.

As the college did not provide any hostel facility, he rented an apartment nearby. One day, he was surprised to meet Parth, his school friend. Parth was studying in his second year and was searching for accommodation near the college premises.

Staying alone was dull and when Anil requested Parth to stay with him, he happily agreed. Parth was a health and fitness enthusiast and advocated a happy and peaceful life. As the place where they were staying was not a very happening one, Anil started joining Parth for jogging, exercising, and yoga. Even though Anil's mother had equipped the kitchen with all the latest gadgets, Anil was not inclined toward cooking. The lack of good eateries nearby left them with no choice but to survive on the food cooked by Bala, their caretaker.

One fine morning, while jogging Anil recollected their old days, "City life is so vibrant, and we have grab-and-go convenience food available everywhere. Frequently, I used to have something yummy- pizza, burger, Franky, doughnut...." Parth, who was obsessed with healthy eating cheered him, "Junk food is high in calories and low in nutritional value which leads to obesity, learning problems, and depression. We are what we eat – physically and mentally. People who eat healthy foods are happier than those addicted to junk food. We should not consume food just for momentary pleasures but for lifelong health and happiness. Occasionally, you can indulge yourself and party hard."

On the way back home, they bought cheese and pizza base from a supermarket. Parth requested Anil to grate the cheese while he quickly chopped capsicums, tomatoes, and onions. Anil was amazed to see his friend chopping vegetables so finely, "Dude, you cut vegetables like a professional chef." Parth spread the sauce on the pizza base, sprinkled cheese, added the vegetable toppings, and put the dish in the oven to bake. He then told his story, "After I lost my mother to cancer, I started assisting my father in the kitchen. My father is an excellent cook and he taught me everything from chopping to cooking." Both of them relished the delicious pizza. With the cheese melting in his mouth, Anil told him about his childhood obsession with pizzas. Every weekend they would make grilled sandwiches, and Frankies and try several new recipes.

Anil lost a lot of weight by regularly exercising and eating healthy food. He looked handsome and happy and felt more active and energetic than before. When his parents visited him, they were pleasantly surprised to see their son in such good shape, radiating peace and happiness. Anil introduced them to his friend Parth and seeing the admiration in their eyes told them about his magical transformation. "Both of you were always worried about my food habits. I used to eat only those foods that gave me pleasure but were not good for my health. Thanks to my friend Parth, I have learned that eating the right food is the best way to stay healthy and happy. Food that brings pleasure does not necessarily bring happiness."

His father praised both of them for managing their studies and home so well. His mother gave a very enlightening example, "It is always a pleasure to have an ice cream which may not be good for health. But people refrain from consuming gooseberry even though it offers many health benefits." Her husband agreed, "Pleasure is achieved with substance, experienced alone whereas happiness cannot be achieved with substances and experienced in groups."

Facts And Opinions

Excited about his school picnic, Parth was unable to sleep. In the adjacent room, his father, Lokesh stared at the ceiling, struggling to get a few winks of sleep. Monstrous thoughts of all dimensions were breeding in his evil mind. His beautiful wife, Sujatha was fast asleep. She had a hectic day at work and then had to pick up the necessary goods for the picnic on her way back home. She was looking radiant in the gentle nightlight. Lokesh was a chartered accountant known for his amiable disposition. He had never raised his voice on his wife or son. But today, he wanted to annihilate his wife. He had browsed through a few crime stories and chalked out his plan, "I cannot see her suffer. So, I will first sedate her and then throttle her. Tomorrow is the perfect day as Parth won't be around." He was sweating profusely, and his heart started pounding. Shivering from head to toe, he got up and sent a message to Akash, "Let us meet tomorrow. It is urgent." Akash, Lokesh, and Sujatha were childhood friends.

The next day, after dropping Parth off at school, Lokesh and Sujatha went to their respective workplaces. Lokesh was unable to focus on his work. He had ambivalent feelings towards Sujatha and did not trust his instincts. He met Akash at a coffee shop and poured out his heart to him. Akash simply stared at Lokesh, surprised and aghast. Then he threw up his hands in horror and questioned Lokesh, "How can you think about Sujatha in that fashion? She is like a sister to me.

Sujatha was seen with a young lad by some distant cousin of yours and she is spreading rumors about her, and you are worried about the people's opinion about her. Most opinions are without value because they are based on guesswork and hearsay evidence. Drifters who are dealing with their failures and frustrations usually have an assortment of opinions about everything you can imagine. Don't be so quick to believe what you hear, because lies spread faster than the truth. Sujatha is mature beyond her age and will never ruin her promising career. There is a huge difference in what appears to people and what is happening."

Akash was concerned and worried about Sujatha. Lokesh was so disgusted and livid, that he did not feel like leaving him alone. As his wife had gone on an official trip, he could spend the whole evening with his bewildered friend. Sujatha was a talented interior designer working for a design studio, 'Interior Point'. She was quite popular among the clients for her eclectic sense of design. His boss was hospitalized in a nursing home next to Interior Point. So, he chalked out a plan that they would visit their boss and then catch up with Sujatha. On reaching Sujatha's office, they were told by the receptionist that she was giving a presentation to her clients. Sujatha's close friend, Alka left a message for her and took them to the office canteen. Feeling a bit awkward, Lokesh said, "Actually, Akash was coming in this direction to see his boss and he dragged me along." Alka never felt that she was meeting Lokesh for the first time as she had already heard so much about him from Sujatha. Unlike men, women share their personal experiences. Alka, "Sujatha is always praising you for your support and cooperation without which it would not have been possible for her to work with a small kid."

Meanwhile, Sujatha had finished her presentation. Her work was appreciated both by the client and her boss. She joined them in the canteen, accompanied by a young lad in his twenties. After the initial introductions got over, Nabil looked at Lokesh admiringly, "Good Afternoon Sir. I have heard so much about you from Sujatha Madam. Pleased to meet you in person today." Sujatha praised Nabil for his proficiency in various design software and digital photography. Sujatha ordered sandwiches for all of them. She had been entrusted with the responsibility of doing the interiors of luxurious, fully furnished apartments in a high-end residential building. "I am so happy and excited that my design proposal has been approved by the client. I am highly indebted to Nabil for making such impressive visuals.". Then she requested Akash, "Without Parth, the house will wear a deserted look. Akash, why don't you come home with us."

After spending a few hours at their home, they went out for dinner. Lokesh was feeling awkward and remained silent. It was only Sujatha who did the talking, "We have been given the contract for doing interiors for a newly constructed building. Nowadays, builders are offering fully furnished luxurious apartments with all modern amenities. Owing to the ongoing construction work, the road connecting the building to the highway is in pathetic condition. So, I park my car in a nearby mall and visit the site with Nabil on his bike. That reminds me, Nabil is getting married to his girlfriend next Sunday. Lokesh, we must attend his wedding."

All these discussions exculpated Sujatha and her husband went red with shame. He felt grateful and indebted to Akash for averting a major tragedy in his life. That brought back his memory of a similar incident when his sister was pursuing her doctorate under a senior professor. Her guide, a pervert used to make advances on her, and the poor girl did not know how to react. She was only interested in academics, and he then defamed her. Frustrated and feeling helpless, she quit the program. Sujatha was tired and wanted to go home and relax. After dropping her home, the two friends went for a drive. Akash laid stress on the fact that suspicion in marriage is the worst possible crisis that pushes the relationship to the brink of failure. Suspicion can snowball into criminal acts. He picked up the newspaper lying on the backseat and read aloud, "Man kills wife for suspecting him of having an illicit affair". "Suspecting wife's fidelity, man kills wife, two children". Every day, newspapers report two or three unpleasant, hair-raising macabre incidents, and most of them are carried out in a fit of rage only to repent later.

Lokesh agreed, "Women have evolved and liberated themselves. They have carved a niche for themselves in every sphere of life. The need of the hour is for the men to be liberated. It is only the insecure men who are distrustful of their wives 'professional friendliness with the opposite sex. Why can't two individuals be good friends without being in a relationship". In a lighter vein, Akash said that even the mother-in-law is no longer considered a monster-in-law anymore. She is a modern, working woman who believes in empowering her bahu. Now, it is for men to change their outlook. Even for one day, men cannot multitask like them-juggling family and professional responsibilities. Finally, they reached Akash's house. While alighting from the car, he gave his final piece of wisdom, "Whenever you hear someone talking maliciously, try to find the source of information.

Look into their eyes and ask a simple, straightforward question -How do you know? Follow this principle and you will be saved from many tragedies in your life."

Best Friend

Eager to meet her friends, Snow-white was excitedly scrambling towards the park. Looking adorable in her white shining coat with a red ribbon across her neck, she surely was a head-turner. She found it quite amusing to see little kids going to the children's playground accompanied by their parents, grandparents, and maids, carrying water-bottle and a bag. She wondered, "Are they going to the park or some evening school?" Some people could be found jogging with headphones and their mobiles secured on their armbands. She felt glad that she could pitter-patter without any of these accessories.

On reaching the park, she found her friends, Bella and Stella already waiting for her. After a quick exchange of greetings, they jetted off on a race across the park and then relaxed under a shady tree. Her friends glanced at her admiringly, "You look lovely today." Blushing coyly, Snowy replied, "Today is my birthday. Last year, I was given as a birthday gift to Neha. She was so excited to see me- a small, white puppy in a red basket and shrieked in excitement- Snow-white. My Snowy." Her friends wished her a special day.

Snow-white shared her experience of her first visit to the parlor, "The environment was very calm and relaxing. I was pampered from the tip of the toe to the folds of ears." Sensing her friends' inquisitiveness, she then briefly explained to them, "First they brushed out the loose, dead coat. Then they gave me a warm bath with a luxurious shampoo. After that, I was blow-dried, and my coat was gently brushed." Showing her painted nails, she elaborated, "They trimmed and polished my nails, cleaned my ears and eyes, and also gave me a massage. Overall, it was a rejuvenating experience." Bella and Stella, both aged six years admired the advancements in pet care, but they preferred to be groomed at home. Then they discussed that even though gadgets and gizmos have reduced work pressure on humans, it is surprising that family members hardly spend quality time together.

With a woebegone expression, Bella reminisced, "A few years back, I used to watch cartoon serials with Shalini after she returned home from school. I miss watching Tom and Jerry, Popeye, and Pokémon. Nowadays, everybody is locked in their rooms and gawping at their phones or laptop. Shalini even carries the mobile phone to the rest room and loud music blares out from her Bluetooth speaker."

All of them chuckled when Snowy innocently said, "If Neha is not able to locate her cell phone, she becomes so restless as if she has been put off her life support system. I usually snuggle up in her lap and she strokes me gently while working on her cell phone or laptop." Stella highlighted a few advantages of the mobile phone, "Last week, Archana and her parents had gone for a holiday. Since I was alone with the servants, they used to video call me every day. The screen was so small that I could barely recognize them. But it felt good to listen to their voices."

While the canine friends were discussing the impact of technology on their lives, their young owners indulged in their girl talk. They wished Neha a Happy birthday. Neha also shared her thoughts, "Since my grandfather passed away last month, there won't be any birthday celebrations this year. But I bought some gifts for Snowy. Snowy is always so happy with whatever I get for it -toys, bones, and treats. I enjoy shopping for her, but I find it so hard to shop for other people. It is just impossible to please everyone."

Shalini agreed, "When it is time for me to return home from school, Bella will stand at the gate waiting for me. She is so excited to see me back and gives me such a warm welcome. In the evening also, she wakes me up and fetches my shoes indicating that she wants to go to the park."

In low whispers, Archana told them, "In my building, one dog named Rocky had been diagnosed with depression." Neha exclaimed, "Do dogs also get depressed? How did the owners learn about it?" Archana replied, "He became silent, went off food, and was always yawning and lip licking. During the pandemic, all the family members were at home, and he enjoyed being under the spotlight. They used to walk him, play with him and take him for car rides. Post covid, all the family members started going out and became busy in their daily routine and he felt neglected."

Archana agreed, "This is a matter of concern. Nowadays people are so obsessed with their mobile phones that their pets have started feeling neglected and lonely. Dogs understand us very well and try to cheer us up when we are feeling low. Unfortunately, we are not good at reading them. If we run and play with our dogs, then we need not sweat out in the gym." As it was getting dark, the girls called out for their fur friends back and they walked them home. On the way, they discussed how they would spend more time with their pets and be involved with their lives.

At one time, the dog was considered man's best friend. But now it has slid down to the second position while the first position has been bagged by cell phones. Now, we should take off our attention from our palm pals and make our paw pals our best friends.

www.ingramcontent.com/pod-product-compliance
Lightning Source LLC
LaVergne TN
LVHW061557070526
838199LV00077B/7085